QUICK SKILLS
First Grade

The (sun) is bright!

Carson Dellosa Education
Greensboro, NC

Carson Dellosa Education
PO Box 35665
Greensboro, NC 27425 USA

ISBN 978-1-4838-6823-3

01-261237784

TABLE OF CONTENTS

Name _____

Alphabet Action

Directions: Practice writing the letters.

Aa

Bb

Cc

Dd

Ee

Ff

Gg

Hh

Ii

Alphabet Action

Jj

Kk

Ll

Mm

Nn

Oo

Pp

Qq

Rr

Name _____

Alphabet Action

Ss --

Tt --

Uu --

Vv --

Ww --

Xx --

Yy --

Zz --

Consonant Roundup: B, C, D, F

Beginning consonants are the consonant sounds that come at the beginning of words. Consonants are the letters b, c, d, f, g, h, j, k, l, m, n, p, q, r, s, t, v, w, x, y, and z.

Directions: Say the name of each letter. Say the sound each letter makes. Circle the letters that make the **beginning** sound for each picture.

Bb	**Cc**	**Dd**	**Ff**

Bb Dd	Ff Cc	Cc Dd	Ff Bb

Bb Dd	Ff Cc	Cc Dd	Ff Bb

Name _____

Consonant Roundup: G, H, J, K

Directions: Say the name of each letter. Say the sound each letter makes. Draw a line from each letter pair to the picture that begins with that sound.

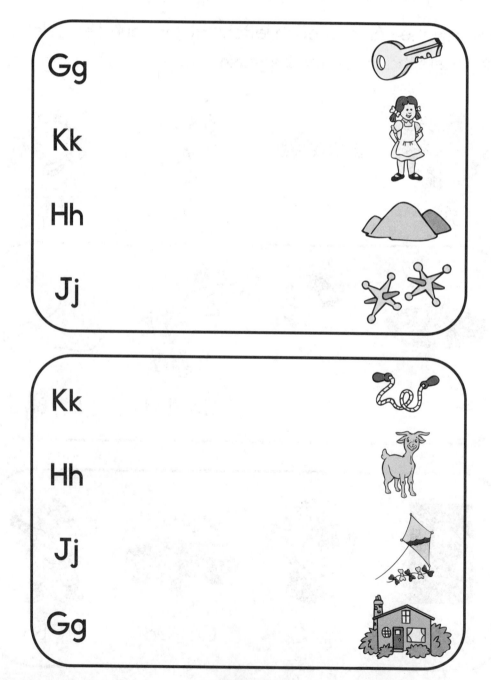

Gg

Kk

Hh

Jj

Kk

Hh

Jj

Gg

Consonant Roundup: L, M, N, P

Directions: Say the name of each letter. Say the sound each letter makes. Trace the letter pair that makes the beginning sound in each picture.

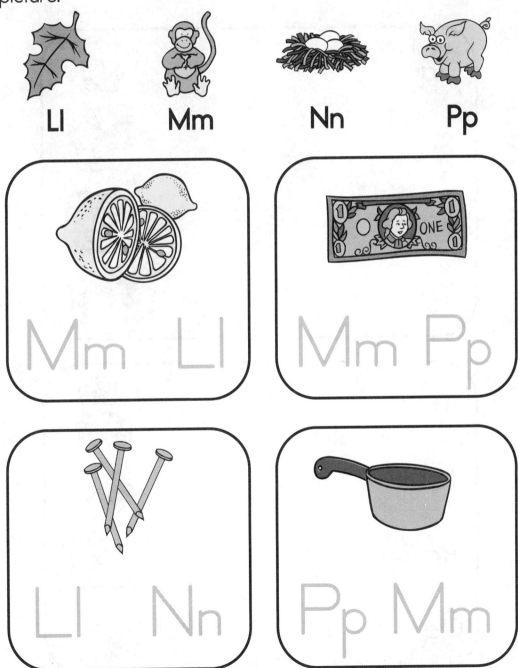

Name _____

Consonant Roundup: Q, R, S, T

Directions: Say the name of each letter. Say the sound each letter makes. Draw a line from each letter pair to the picture that begins with that sound.

Consonant Roundup: V, W, X, Y, Z

Directions: Say the name of each letter. Say the sound that each letter makes. Draw a line from each letter pair to the picture that begins with that sound.

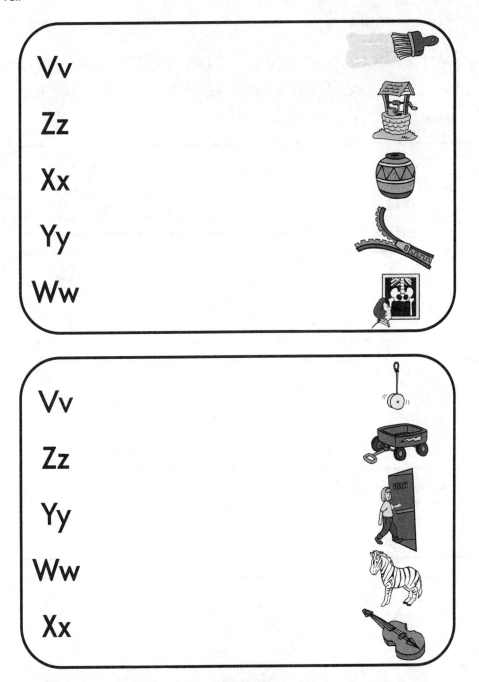

Name _____

Say It Short

Vowels are the letters **a, e, i, o,** and **u.** Short **a** is the sound you hear in **ant.** Short **e** is the sound you hear in **elephant.** Short **i** is the sound you hear in **igloo.** Short **o** is the sound you hear in **octopus.** Short **u** is the sound you hear in **umbrella.**

Directions: Say the short vowel sound at the beginning of each row. Say the name of each picture. Then, color the pictures that have the same short vowel sounds as that letter.

Say It Short

Directions: In each box are three pictures. The words that name the pictures have missing letters. Write **a, e, i, o,** or **u** to finish the words.

p___n

p___n

p___n

b___g

b___g

b___g

c___t

c___t

c___t

h___t

h___t

h___t

Name _____

Say It Long

Vowels are the letters **a, e, i, o,** and **u.** Long vowel sounds say their own names. Long **a** is the sound you hear in **hay.** Long **e** is the sound you hear in **me.** Long **i** is the sound you hear in **pie.** Long **o** is the sound you hear in **no.** Long **u** is the sound you hear in **cute.**

Directions: Say the long vowel sound at the beginning of each row. Say the name of each picture. Color the pictures in each row that have the same long vowel sound as that letter.

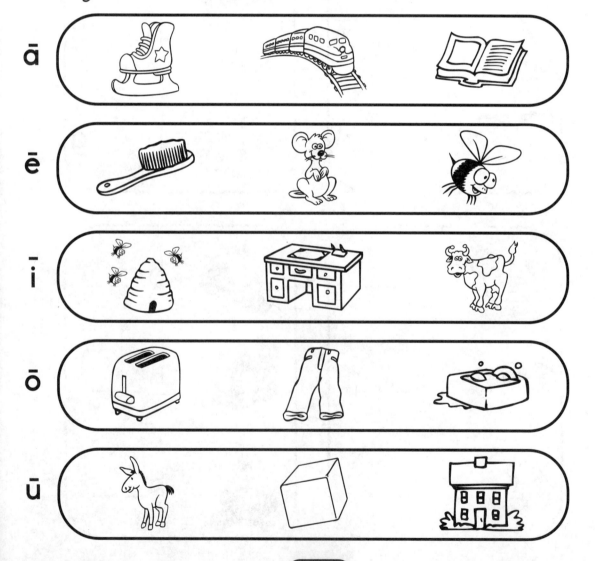

ā

ē

ī

ō

ū

Say It Long

Directions: Write **a**, **e**, **i**, **o**, or **u** in each blank to finish the word. Draw a line from the word to the picture.

c＿ke

r＿se

k＿te

f＿＿t

m＿le

Name _____

Review

Directions: Write the vowel on each line that completes the word.

a   e   i   o   u

c___t

b___k___

sm___k___

tr___ ___

d___ck

p___n

m___m

b___b

Review

Directions: Circle the **long vowel** words with a **red** crayon. Underline the **short vowel** words with a **blue** crayon.

Remember: The vowel is long if:

- There are two vowels in the word. The first vowel is the sound you hear.

- There is a "super silent e" at the end.

cub	red	coat
bite	cube	cage
cat	mean	rake
bit	cot	hen
leaf	feet	key
pen	web	bee
nest	boat	fox
rose	dog	pig

Name _____

Begin with a Blend

Consonant blends are two or more consonant sounds together in a word. The blend is made by combining the consonant sounds.

Example: floor

Directions: The name of each picture begins with a **blend**. Circle the beginning blend for each picture.

bl fl cl	cl fl gl	fl bl pl
fl cl gl	pl gl cl	gl fl sl
gl fl cl	sl fl cl	cl gl sl

Blend in the Blank

Directions: The beginning blend for each word is missing. Fill in the correct blend to finish the word. Draw a line from the word to the picture.

_____ain

_____og

_____um

_____ush

_____esent

Name _____

Rhythm and Rhyme

Rhyming words are words that sound alike at the end of the word. **Cat** and **hat** rhyme.

Directions: Draw a circle around each word pair that rhymes. Draw an **X** on each pair that does not rhyme.

Example:

(soap rope)	red dog	book hook
cold rock	cat hat	yellow black
one two	rock sock	rat flat
good nice	you to	meet toy
old sold	sale whale	word letter

Putting Things in Order

Directions: Abc order is the order in which letters come in the alphabet. Circle the first letter of each word. Then, put each pair of words in **abc** order.

©ar   ⓑird

moon   **2** two

bird

car

nest    fan

card    dog

pig    bike

sun    pie

Name _____

Two Words in One

Compound words are two words that are put together to make one new word.

Directions: Look at the pictures and the two words that are next to each other. Put the words together to make a new word. Write the new word.

Example:

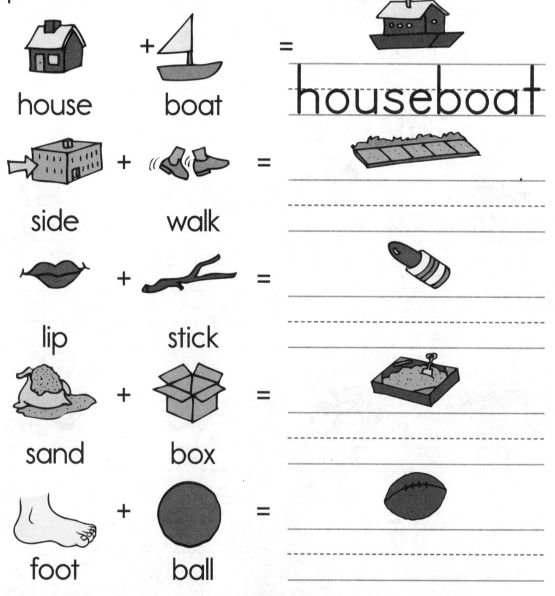

house + boat = houseboat

side + walk = _____

lip + stick = _____

sand + box = _____

foot + ball = _____

The Name Game

You are a special person. Your name begins with a capital letter. We put a capital letter at the beginning of people's names because they are special.

Directions: Write your name. Did you remember to use a capital letter?

_____

- -

_____

Directions: Write each person's name. Use a capital letter at the beginning.

Ted

Katie

Marcos

Tim

Write a friend's name. Use a capital letter at the beginning.

_____

- -

_____

Name _____

7 Delightful Days

The days of the week begin with capital letters.

Directions: Write the days of the week in the spaces below. Put them in order. Be sure to start with capital letters.

Tuesday

Saturday

Monday

Friday

Thursday

Sunday

Wednesday

_____

_____

_____

_____

_____

_____

_____

12 Marvelous Months

The months of the year begin with capital letters.

Directions: Write the months of the year in order on the calendar below. Be sure to use capital letters.

January	July	June	April	November	February
October	December	March	September	May	August

_____

_____

_____

_____

_____

_____

_____

_____

_____

_____

Name _____

Like It or Not

Directions: Circle the picture in each row that is most like the first picture.

Example:

carrot   jacks   bread   pea

baseball   sneakers   basketball   bat

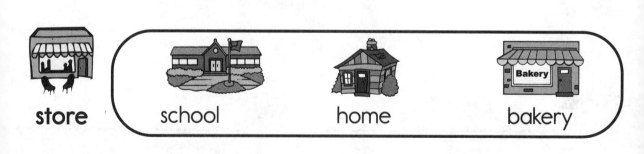

store   school   home   bakery

kitten   dog   fox   cat

Odd One Out

Directions: Draw an **X** on the picture that does not belong in each group.

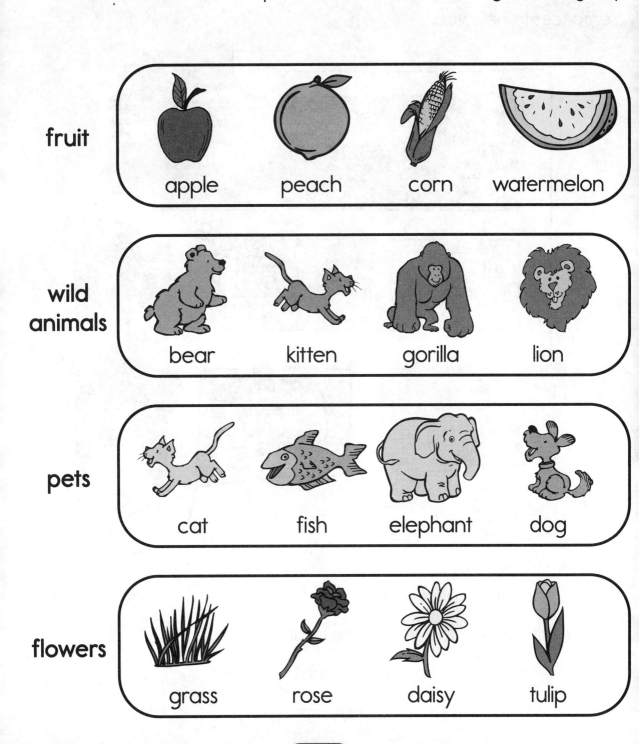

fruit | apple | peach | corn | watermelon

wild animals | bear | kitten | gorilla | lion

pets | cat | fish | elephant | dog

flowers | grass | rose | daisy | tulip

LANGUAGE ARTS

Name _____

Map It!

Directions: Color the path the girl should take to go home. Use the sentences to help you.

1. Go to the school and turn left.

2. At the end of the street, turn right.

3. Walk past the park and turn right.

4. After you pass the pool, turn right.

© Carson Dellosa Education

28

Make a Snowman!

Directions: Write the number of the sentence that goes with each picture in the circle.

1. Roll a large snowball for the snowman's bottom.

2. Make another snowball and put it on top of the first.

3. Put the last snowball on top.

4. Dress the snowman.

Name _____

Puddle Jumping

Directions: Read the story. Write the words from the story that complete each sentence.

Jada and Bill like to play in the rain. They take off their shoes and socks. They splash in the puddles. It feels cold! It is fun to splash!

_____

Jada and Bill like to _____.

_____

They take off their _____.

_____

They splash in _____.

Do you like to splash in puddles?   Yes   No

Falling Leaves

Directions: Read about raking leaves. Then, answer the questions.

I like to rake leaves. Do you? Leaves die each year. They get brown and dry. They fall from the trees. Then, we rake them up.

1. What color are leaves when they die?

   _____

   -

   _____

2. What happens when they die?

   _____

   -

   _____

   -

   _____

3. What do we do when leaves fall?

   _____

   -

   _____

Name _____

Nouns All Around

Directions: Write these naming words in the correct box.

store	zoo	child	baby
teacher	table	cat	park
gym	woman	sock	horse

Person

_____ _____

_____ _____

Place

_____ _____

_____ _____

Thing

_____ _____

_____ _____

Pick a Pair

Some nouns name things that go together.

Directions: Draw a line to match the nouns on the left with the things they go with on the right.

toothpaste

washcloth

pencil

sock

salt

toothbrush

shoe

pepper

soap

paper

pillow

bed

Name _____

Get in on the Action

Directions: Look at the picture and read the words. Write an action word in each sentence below.

1. The two boys like to _____ together.

2. The children _____ the soccer ball.

3. Some children like to _____ on the swing.

4. The girl can _____ very fast.

5. The teacher _____ the bell.

Review

Directions: Read the sentences below. Draw a **red** circle around the nouns. Draw a **blue** line under the verbs.

1. The boy runs fast.

2. The turtle eats leaves.

3. The fish swim in the tank.

4. The girl hits the ball.

Name _____

Show and Tell

Directions: Read the words in the box. Choose the word that describes the picture. Write it next to the picture.

wet   round   funny   soft   sad   tall

 _____

 _____

 _____

 _____

 _____

 _____

Picture Perfect

Colors and numbers can describe nouns.

Directions: Underline the describing word in each sentence. Draw a picture to go with each sentence.

A yellow moon was in the sky.

Two worms are on the road.

The tree had red apples.

The girl wore a blue dress.

Name _____

1, 2, 3—Compare and See

Directions: Look at the pictures in each row. Write 1, 2, or 3 under the pictures to put them in order.

Example:

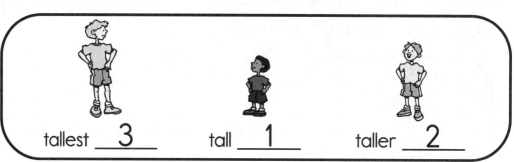

tallest __3__   tall __1__   taller __2__

small _____   smallest _____   smaller _____

biggest _____   big _____   bigger _____

wider _____   wide _____   widest _____

1, 2, 3—Compare and See

Directions: Look at the pictures in each row. Write 1, 2, or 3 under the pictures to put them in order.

shortest _____   shorter _____   short _____

longest _____   longer _____   long _____

happy _____   happier _____   happiest _____

hotter _____   hot _____   hottest _____

Name _____

Synonym Sense

Synonyms are words that mean almost the same thing. **Start** and **begin** are synonyms.

Directions: Find the synonyms that describe each picture. Write the words in the boxes next to the picture.

small	funny	large	sad
silly	little	unhappy	big

_____ _____

_____ _____

_____ _____

_____ _____

All About Antonyms

Antonyms are words that are opposites. **Hot** and **cold** are antonyms.

Directions: Draw a line between the antonyms.

closed

below

full

empty

above

old

new

open

Name _____

Sound Alikes

Homophones are words that **sound** the same but are spelled differently and mean something different. **Blew** and **blue** are homophones.

Directions: Look at the word pairs. Choose the word that describes the picture. Write the word on the line next to the picture.

1. sew   so   _____

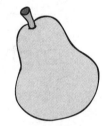

2. pair   pear   _____

3. eye   I   _____

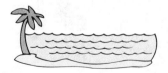

4. see   sea   _____

Say it with a Sentence

Sentences begin with capital letters.

Directions: Read the sentences and write them below. Begin each sentence with a capital letter.

Example:

the cat is fat.

$$\overline{\text{The cat is fat.}}$$

my dog is big.

the boy is sad.

bikes are fun!

dad can bake.

Name _____

Telling Sentences: Pet Crazy

Directions: Read the sentences and write them below. Begin each sentence with a capital letter. End each sentence with a period.

1. most children like pets
2. some children like dogs
3. some children like cats
4. some children like snakes
5. some children like all animals

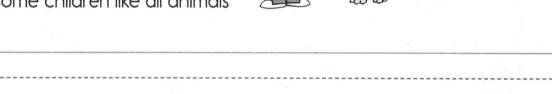

1. _____

2. _____

3. _____

4. _____

5. _____

Asking Sentences: Monkeying Around

Directions: Write the first word of each asking sentence. Be sure to begin each question with a capital letter. End each question with a question mark.

1. _____ you like the zoo   do

2. _____ much does it cost   how

3. _____ you feed the ducks   can

4. _____ you see the monkeys   will

5. _____ time will you eat lunch   what

Name _____

Hop to It!

Directions: How many are there of each picture? Write the answers in the boxes. The first one is done for you.

Number Names

Directions: Match the correct number of objects with the number. Then, match the number with the word.

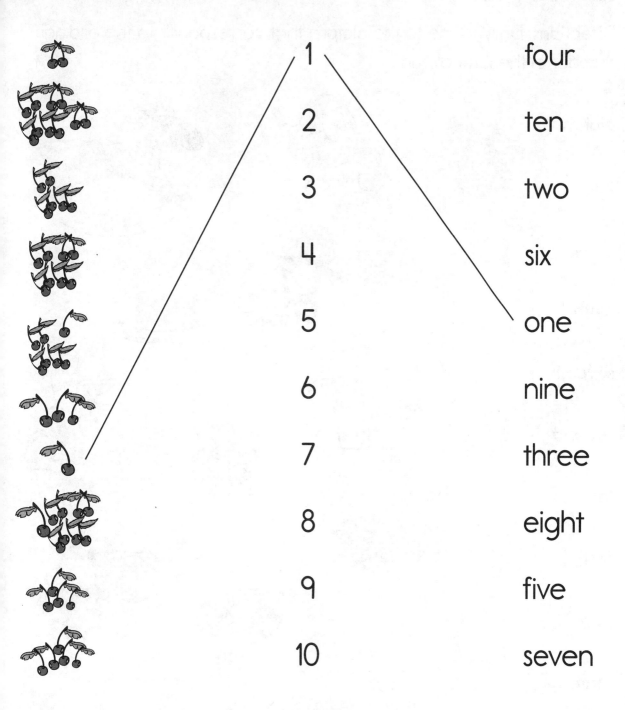

1	four
2	ten
3	two
4	six
5	one
6	nine
7	three
8	eight
9	five
10	seven

Name _____

Ordinal Animals

Ordinal numbers are used to indicate order in a series, such as **first**, **second**, or **third**.

Directions: Draw a line to the picture that corresponds to the ordinal number in the left column.

eighth

third

sixth

ninth

seventh

second

fourth

first

fifth

tenth

1st

7th

10th

2nd

4th

6th

8th

9th

5th

3rd

48

Add It Up!

Directions: Draw the correct number of dots next to the numbers in each problem. Add up the number of dots to find your answer.

Example:

$$3 \bullet\bullet\bullet$$
$$\underline{+\ 2} \ \bullet\bullet$$

$$2 + 2 = \underline{\quad}$$
$$\bullet\bullet \quad \bullet\bullet$$

$$4$$
$$\underline{+\ 2}$$

$$1 + 5 = \underline{\quad}$$

$$3$$
$$\underline{+\ 1}$$

$$4 + 3 = \underline{\quad}$$

$$6$$
$$\underline{+\ 2}$$

$$5 + 3 = \underline{\quad}$$

MATH

Name _____

In the Doghouse

Directions: Add the numbers. Put your answers in the doghouses.

Example: 4 + 2 = 6

2 + 6 =

7 + 3 =

6 + 1 =

4 + 5 =

6 + 2 =

7 + 2 =

© Carson Dellosa Education

Name _____

Fresh and Fruity

Directions: Count the fruit in each bowl. Write your answers in the blanks. Circle the problem that matches your answer.

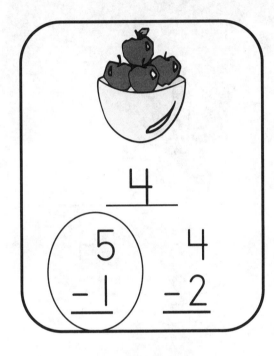

$$\frac{}{4}$$

$$\frac{5}{-1}\qquad \frac{4}{-2}$$

$$\frac{}{}$$

$$\frac{3}{-0}\qquad \frac{4}{-2}$$

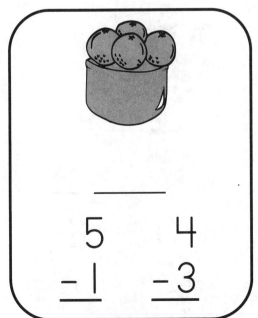

$$\frac{}{}$$

$$\frac{5}{-1}\qquad \frac{4}{-3}$$

$$\frac{}{}$$

$$\frac{3}{-2}\qquad \frac{5}{-0}$$

Name _____

Flower Power

Directions: Count the flowers. Write your answers in the blanks. Circle the problem that matches your answer.

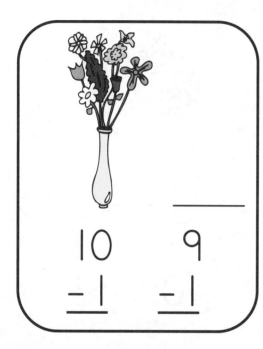

$$10 \\ -1$$ $$9 \\ -1$$

$$7 \\ -2$$ $$9 \\ -3$$

$$9 \\ -6$$ $$8 \\ -0$$

$$10 \\ -2$$ $$8 \\ -1$$

Solve It!

Directions: Solve the problems. Remember, addition means "putting together," or adding, two or more numbers to find the sum. Subtraction means "taking away," or subtracting, one number from another.

1 + 3 = ___   4 – 3 = ___   4 + 5 = ___

6 + 1 = ___   7 – 2 = ___   8 – 4 = ___

9 – 1 = ___   10 – 3 = ___

5 – 2 = ___   6 + 3 = ___

8 + 2 = ___   5 + 5 = ___

Review

Directions: Trace the numbers. Work the problems.

1 2 3 4 5 6 7 8 9 10

$$\begin{array}{r} 9 \\ -3 \\ \hline \end{array}$$

$$\begin{array}{r} 6 \\ +2 \\ \hline \end{array}$$

$$\begin{array}{r} 3 \\ +4 \\ \hline \end{array}$$

$$\begin{array}{r} 5 \\ +4 \\ \hline \end{array}$$

$$\begin{array}{r} 9 \\ -5 \\ \hline \end{array}$$

$$\begin{array}{r} 7 \\ +2 \\ \hline \end{array}$$

$$\begin{array}{r} 4 \\ -2 \\ \hline \end{array}$$

$$\begin{array}{r} 6 \\ +3 \\ \hline \end{array}$$

$$\begin{array}{r} 9 \\ -7 \\ \hline \end{array}$$

Know Your Place

The place value of a digit, or numeral, is shown by where it is in the number. For example, in the number **23**, **2** has the place value of **tens**, and **3** is **ones**.

Directions: Count the groups of ten crayons and write the number by the word **tens**. Count the other crayons and write the number by the word **ones**.

Example: [crayons] + [crayon] = __1__ ten + __1__ one

[crayons] + [crayons] = ____ tens + ____ ones

[crayons] + [crayons] = ____ tens + ____ ones

[crayons] + [crayon] = ____ tens + ____ ones

6 tens + 3 ones = ____   5 tens + 1 one = ____

3 tens + 8 ones = ____   9 tens + 7 ones = ____

4 tens + 5 ones = ____   2 tens + 8 ones = ____

Name _____

Counting on Crayons

Directions: Circle groups of ten crayons. Add the remaining ones to make the correct number.

tens   ones

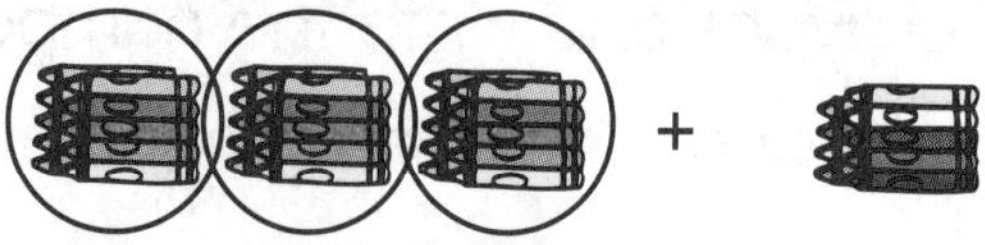

+ = $\underline{3}$ $\underline{9}$

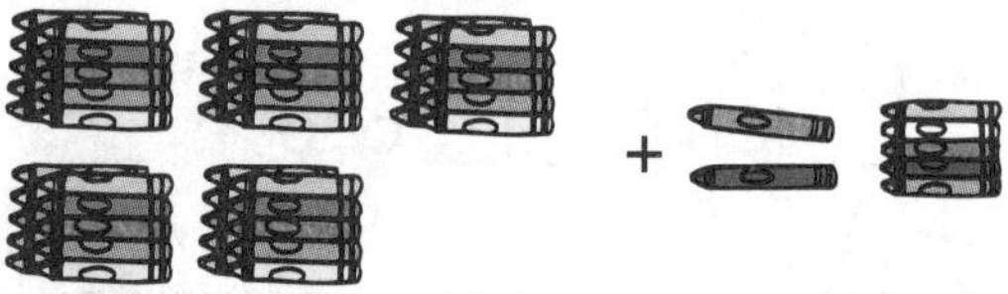

+ = ___ ___

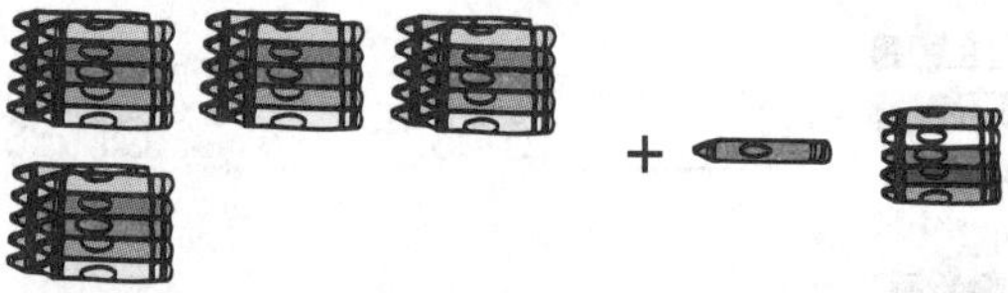

+ = ___ ___

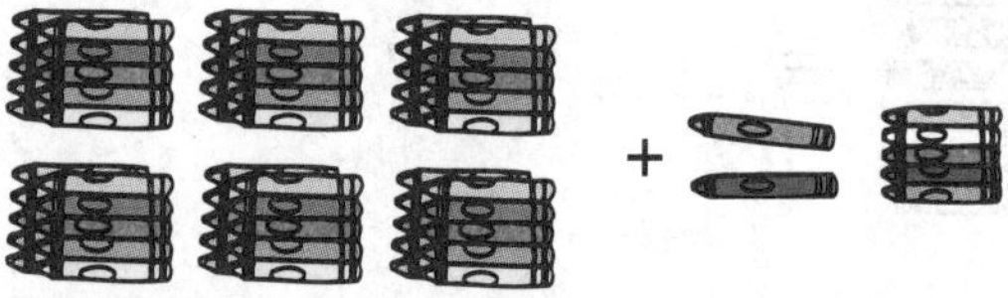

+ = ___ ___

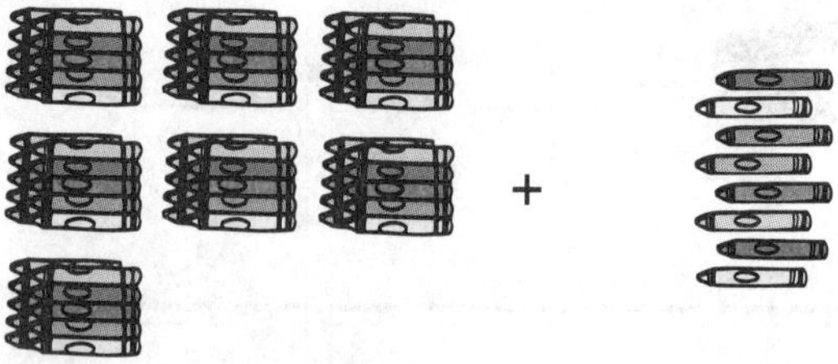

+ = ___ ___

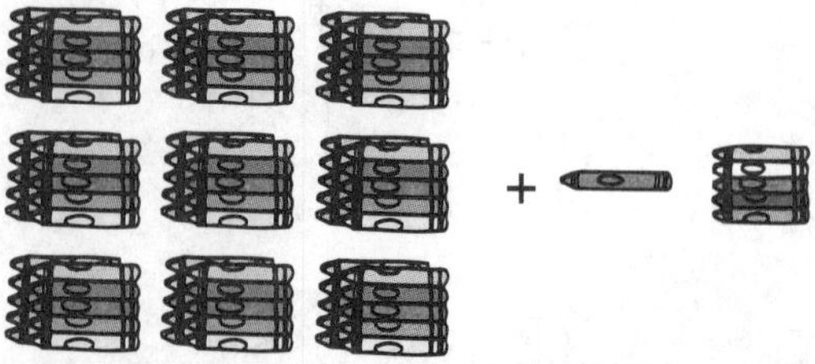

+ = ___ ___

6 + 6 = ___   8 + 4 = ___   9 + 5 = ___

Crayon Cross-out

Directions: Count the crayons in each group. Put an **X** through the number of crayons being subtracted. How many are left?

$-\ 5\ =\ \underline{10}$

$-\ 4\ =\ \underline{\quad}$

$-\ 7\ =\ \underline{\quad}$

$-\ 6\ =\ \underline{\quad}$

$-\ 5\ =\ \underline{\quad}$

$-\ 8\ =\ \underline{\quad}$

$13 - 8 =$ ___ $11 - 5 =$ ___ $12 - 9 =$ ___

$14 - 7 =$ ___ $10 - 7 =$ ___ $13 - 3 =$ ___

$15 - 9 =$ ___ $11 - 8 =$ ___ $12 - 10 =$ ___

Name _____

Fair and Square

A square is a figure with four corners and four sides of the same length. This is a square ☐.

Directions: Find the squares and circle them.

Directions: Trace the word. Write the word.

square

58

Circles All Around

A circle is a figure that is round. This is a circle ◯.

Directions: Find the circles and put a square around them.

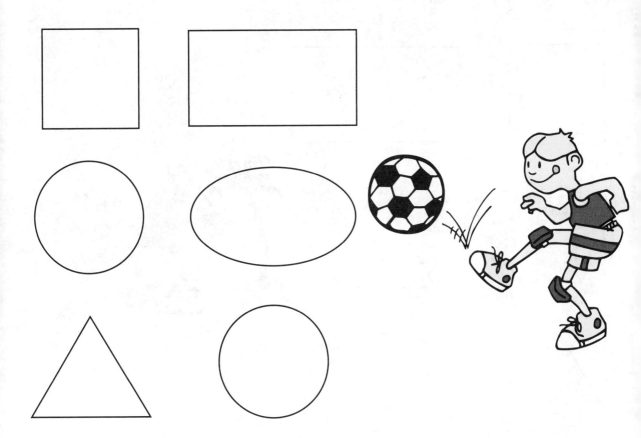

Directions: Trace the word. Write the word.

circle

Name _____

Totally Triangles

A triangle is a figure with three corners and three sides. This is a triangle △.

Directions: Find the triangles and put a circle around them.

Directions: Trace the word. Write the word.

triangle

Make Room for Rectangles

A rectangle is a figure with four corners and four sides. Sides opposite each other are the same length. This is a rectangle ▭.

Directions: Find the rectangles and put a circle around them.

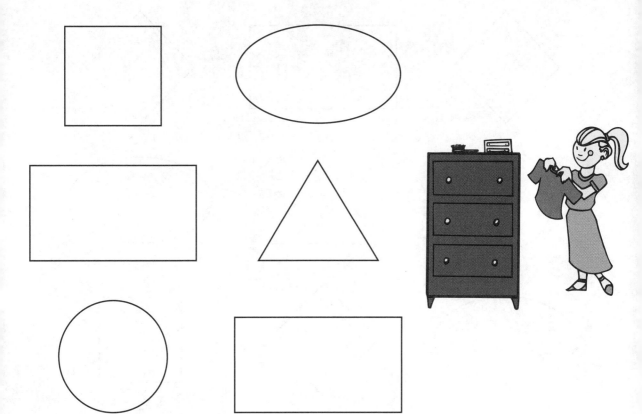

Directions: Trace the word. Write the word.

rectangle

Ovals and Rhombuses

An oval is an egg-shaped figure. A rhombus is a figure with four sides of the same length. It's corners form points at the top, sides, and bottom. This is an oval ⬭. This is a rhombus ◇.

Directions: Color the ovals **red**. Color the rhombuses **blue**.

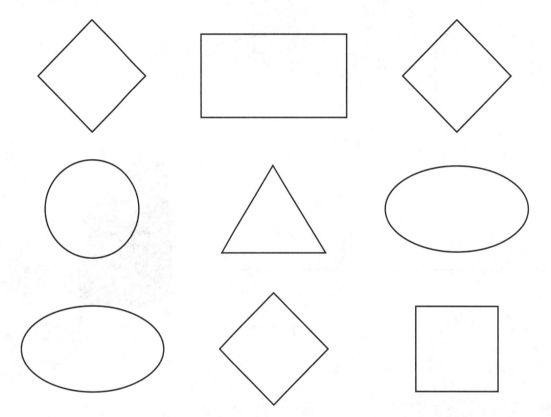

Directions: Trace the word. Write the word.

oval

rhombus

Fraction Action: Whole and Half

A fraction is a number that names part of a whole, such as $\frac{1}{2}$ or $\frac{3}{4}$.

Directions: Color half of each object.

Example:

Whole apple

Half an apple

$\frac{1}{2}$

Name _____

Fraction Action: Thirds and Fourths

Directions: Each object has 3 equal parts. Color one section.

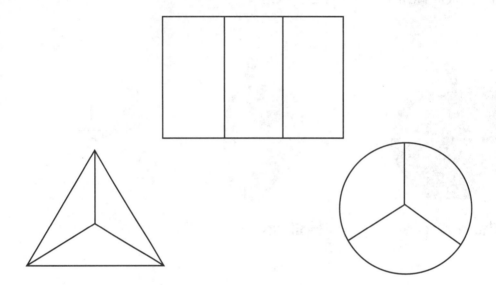

Directions: Each object has 4 equal parts. Color one section.

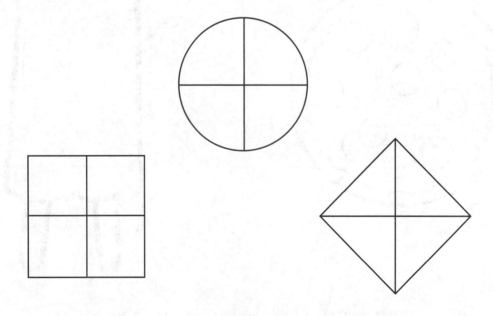

Right on Time!

The short hand of the clock tells the hour. The long hand tells how many minutes after the hour. When the minute hand is on the **12**, it is the beginning of the hour.

Directions: Look at each clock. Write the time.

Example:

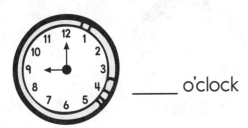

___3___ o'clock

_____ o'clock

_____ o'clock

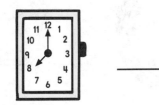

_____ o'clock

_____ o'clock

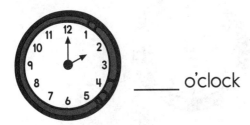

_____ o'clock

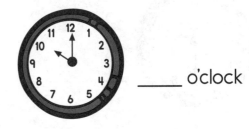

_____ o'clock

Name _____

It's About Time

The short hand of the clock tells the hour. The long hand tells how many minutes after the hour. When the minute hand is on the **6**, it is on the half-hour. A half-hour is thirty minutes. It is written **:30**, such as in **5:30**.

Directions: Look at each clock. Write the time.

Example:

hour   half-hour

__1__ : __30__

 _____ : _____

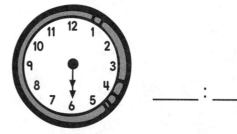 _____ : _____

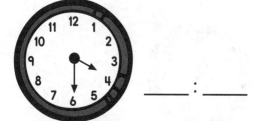 _____ : _____

 _____ : _____

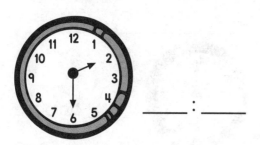 _____ : _____

 _____ : _____

Money Sense

A penny is worth one cent. It is written **1¢** or **$.01**. A nickel is worth five cents. It is written **5¢** or **$.05**. A dime is worth ten cents. It is written **10¢** or **$.10**.

Directions: Add the coins pictured and write the total amounts in the blanks.

Example:

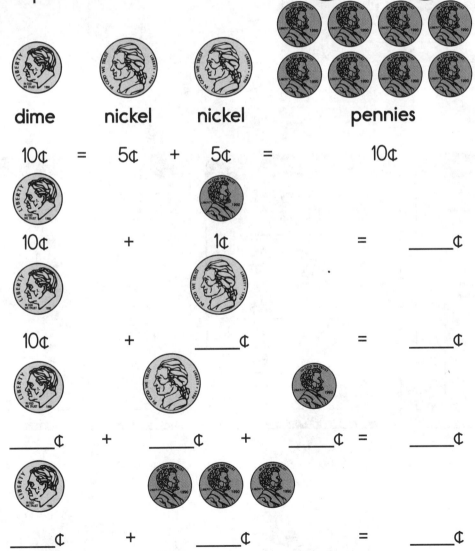

dime		nickel		nickel		pennies
10¢	=	5¢	+	5¢	=	10¢

10¢   +   1¢   =   _____ ¢

10¢   +   _____ ¢   =   _____ ¢

_____ ¢   +   _____ ¢   +   _____ ¢   =   _____ ¢

_____ ¢   +   _____ ¢   =   _____ ¢

ANSWER KEY

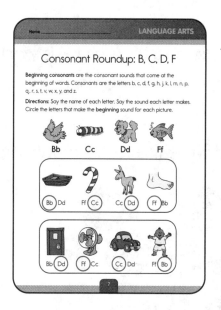

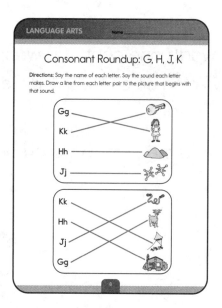

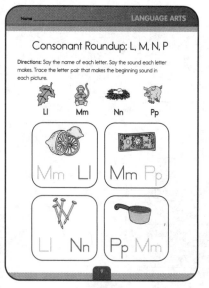

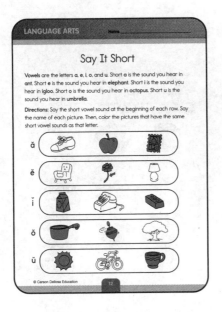

12

13

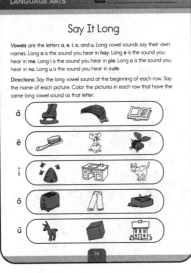

14

15

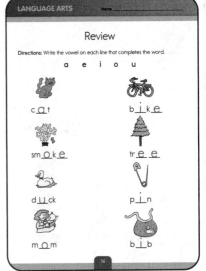

16

ANSWER KEY

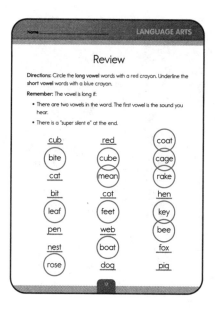

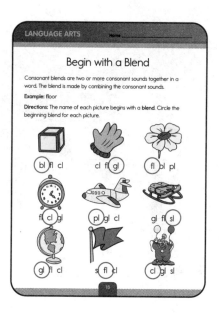

17

18

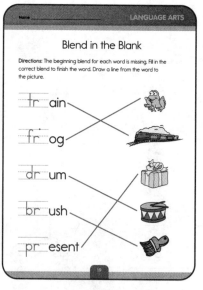

19

20

21

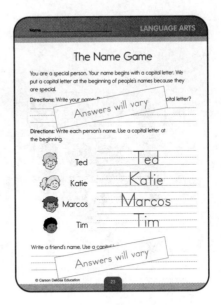

22

23

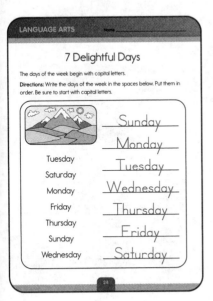

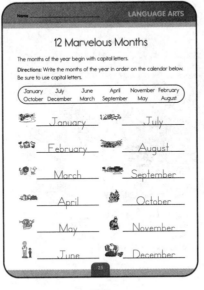

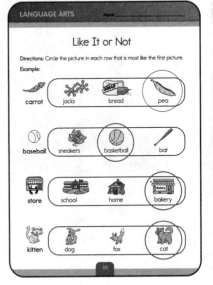

24

25

26

ANSWER KEY

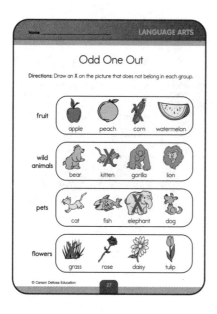

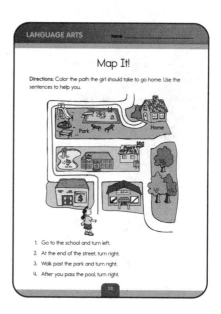

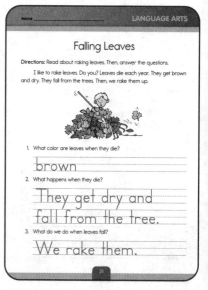

27

28

29

30

31

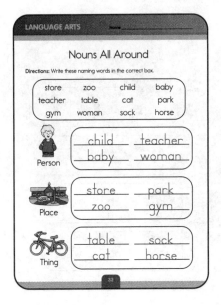

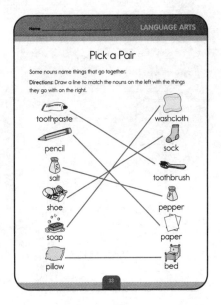

32

33

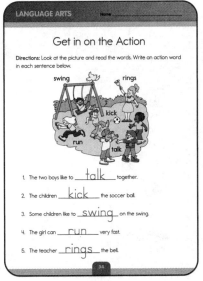

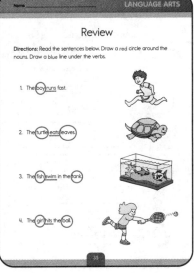

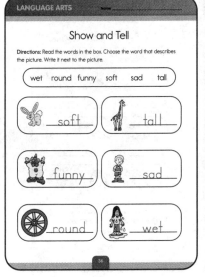

34

35

36

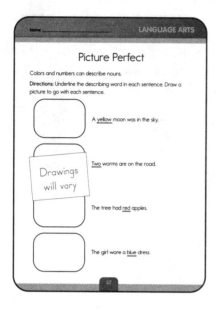

Picture Perfect

Colors and numbers can describe nouns.

Directions: Underline the describing word in each sentence. Draw a picture to go with each sentence.

A <u>yellow</u> moon was in the sky.

<u>Two</u> worms are on the road.

Drawings will vary

The tree had <u>red</u> apples.

The girl wore a <u>blue</u> dress.

37

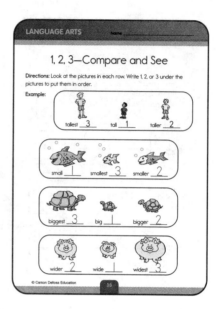

1, 2, 3—Compare and See

Directions: Look at the pictures in each row. Write 1, 2, or 3 under the pictures to put them in order.

Example:

tallest _3_   tall _1_   taller _2_

small _1_   smallest _3_   smaller _2_

biggest _3_   big _1_   bigger _2_

wider _2_   wide _1_   widest _3_

38

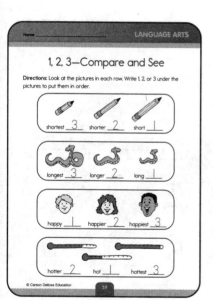

1, 2, 3—Compare and See

Directions: Look at the pictures in each row. Write 1, 2, or 3 under the pictures to put them in order.

shortest _3_   shorter _2_   short _1_

longest _3_   longer _2_   long _1_

happy _1_   happier _2_   happiest _3_

hotter _2_   hot _1_   hottest _3_

39

Synonym Sense

Synonyms are words that mean almost the same thing. **Start** and **begin** are synonyms.

Directions: Find the synonyms that describe each picture. Write the words in the boxes next to the picture.

| small | funny | large | sad |
| silly | little | unhapppy | big |

small   little

large   big

sad   unhappy

funny   silly

40

All About Antonyms

Antonyms are words that are opposites. **Hot** and **cold** are antonyms.

Directions: Draw a line between the antonyms.

closed — open
full — empty
above — below
new — old

41

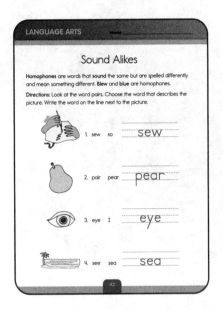

Sound Alikes

Homophones are words that sound the same but are spelled differently and mean something different. **Blew** and **blue** are homophones.

Directions: Look at the word pairs. Choose the word that describes the picture. Write the word on the line next to the picture.

1. sew so   sew
2. pair pear   pear
3. eye I   eye
4. see sea   sea

42

Say it with a Sentence

Sentences begin with capital letters.

Directions: Read the sentences and write them below. Begin each sentence with a capital letter.

Example:

the cat is fat.   The cat is fat.

my dog is big.   My dog is big.

the boy is sad.   The boy is sad.

bikes are fun!   Bikes are fun!

dad can bake.   Dad can bake.

43

Telling Sentences: Pet Crazy

Directions: Read the sentences and write them below. Begin each sentence with a capital letter. End each sentence with a period.

1. most children like pets
2. some children like dogs
3. some children like cats
4. some children like snakes
5. some children like all animals

1. Most children like pets.
2. Some children like dogs.
3. Some children like cats.
4. Some children like snakes.
5. Some children like all animals.

44

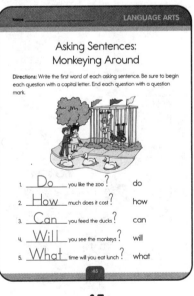

Asking Sentences: Monkeying Around

Directions: Write the first word of each asking sentence. Be sure to begin each question with a capital letter. End each question with a question mark.

1. Do you like the zoo?   do
2. How much does it cost?   how
3. Can you feed the ducks?   can
4. Will you see the monkeys?   will
5. What time will you eat lunch?   what

45

Hop to It!

Directions: How many are there of each picture? Write the answers in the boxes. The first one is done for you.

7
4
10
5
3

46

ANSWER KEY

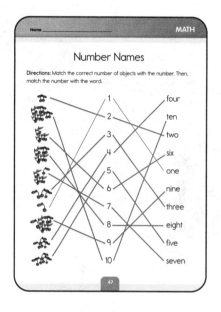

47

48

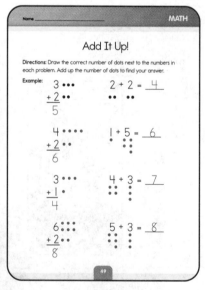

49

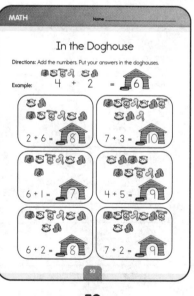

50

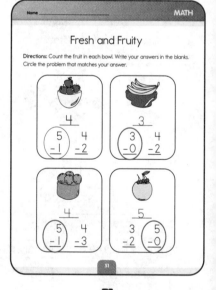

51

© Carson Dellosa Education

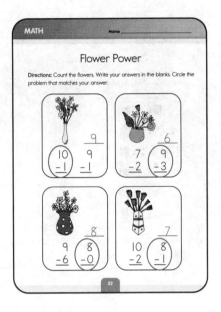

52

Solve It!

Directions: Solve the problems. Remember, addition means "putting together," or adding, two or more numbers to find the sum. Subtraction means "taking away," or subtracting, one number from another.

$1 + 3 = 4$ $4 - 3 = 1$ $4 + 5 = 9$

$6 + 1 = 7$ $7 - 2 = 5$ $8 - 4 = 4$

$9 - 1 = 8$ $10 - 3 = 7$

$5 - 2 = 3$ $6 + 3 = 9$

$8 + 2 = 10$ $5 + 5 = 10$

53

54

Know Your Place

The place value of a digit, or numeral, is shown by where it is in the number. For example, in the number **23, 2** has the place value of **tens**, and **3** is **ones**.

Directions: Count the groups of ten crayons and write the number by the word **tens**. Count the other crayons and write the number by the word **ones**.

Example: ▦ + ▭ = 1 ten + 1 one

▦▦ + ▭▭▭ = 2 tens + 3 ones

▦▦ + ▭▭▭▭ = 4 tens + 8 ones

▦▦ + ▭▭ = 6 tens + 2 ones

6 tens + 3 ones = 63   5 tens + 1 one = 51

3 tens + 8 ones = 38   9 tens + 7 ones = 97

4 tens + 5 ones = 45   2 tens + 8 ones = 28

55

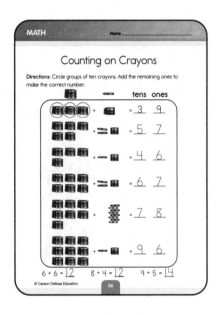

56

Counting on Crayons

Directions: Circle groups of ten crayons. Add the remaining ones to make the correct number.

	tens	ones
	3	9
	5	7
	4	6
	6	7
	7	8
	9	6

6 + 6 = 12   8 + 4 = 12   9 + 5 = 14

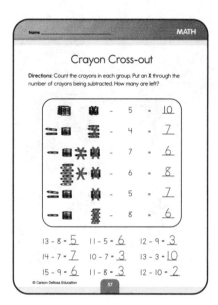

57

Crayon Cross-out

Directions: Count the crayons in each group. Put an X through the number of crayons being subtracted. How many are left?

		- 5	=	10	
		- 4	=	7	
		- 7	=	6	
		- 6	=	8	
		- 5	=	7	
		- 8	=	6	

13 - 8 = 5   11 - 5 = 6   12 - 9 = 3
14 - 7 = 7   10 - 7 = 3   13 - 3 = 10
15 - 9 = 6   11 - 8 = 3   12 - 10 = 2

58

Fair and Square

A square is a figure with four corners and four sides of the same length. This is a square ☐.

Directions: Find the squares and circle them.

Directions: Trace the word. Write the word.

square   square

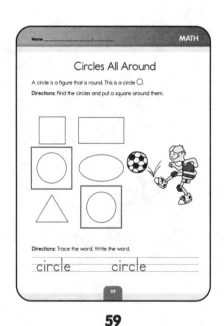

59

Circles All Around

A circle is a figure that is round. This is a circle ○.

Directions: Find the circles and put a square around them.

Directions: Trace the word. Write the word.

circle   circle

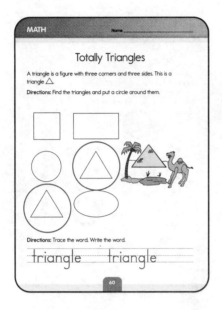

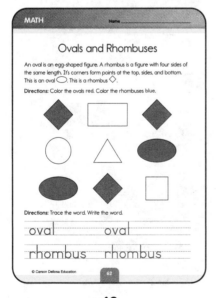

60

61

62

63

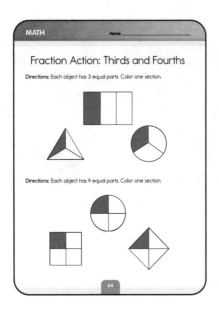

64

Right on Time!

The short hand of the clock tells the hour. The long hand tells how many minutes after the hour. When the minute hand is on the **12**, it is the beginning of the hour.

Directions: Look at each clock. Write the time.

Example:

3 o'clock

9 o'clock   1 o'clock

8 o'clock   5 o'clock

2 o'clock   10 o'clock

65

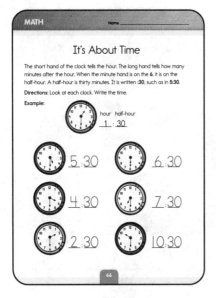

66

Money Sense

A penny is worth one cent. It is written **1¢** or **$.01**. A nickel is worth five cents. It is written **5¢** or **$.05**. A dime is worth ten cents. It is written **10¢** or **$.10**.

Directions: Add the coins pictured and write the total amounts in the blanks.

Example:

dime   nickel   nickel   pennies

10¢   =   5¢   +   5¢   =   10¢

10¢   +   1¢   =   11¢

10¢   +   5¢   =   15¢

10¢   +   5¢   +   1¢   =   16¢

10¢   +   3¢   =   13¢

67